JUNGLE GYM GAMES
Leader Manual

Bible Adventure

Loveland, Colorado

Jungle Gym Games Leader Manual
Copyright © 1999 Group Publishing, Inc.

All rights reserved. No part of this book may be reproduced in any manner whatsoever without prior written permission from the publisher, except where noted on handouts and in the case of brief quotations embodied in critical articles and reviews. For information, write Permissions, Group Publishing, Inc., Dept. PD, P.O. Box 481, Loveland, CO 80539.

Credits
Treasure Hunt Bible Adventure Coordinator: Jody Brolsma
Author: Amy Nappa
Chief Creative Officer: Joani Schultz
Copy Editor: Candace McMahan
Art Director: Kari K. Monson
Cover Art Director: Lisa Chandler
Cover Designers: Becky Hawley and Jerry Krutar
Computer Graphic Artist: Nighthawk Design
Cover Photographer: Craig DeMartino
Illustrator: Amy Bryant
Rain Forest Art: Pat Allen
Rain Forest Art Photographer: Linda Bohm
Production Manager: Peggy Naylor

Unless otherwise noted, Scripture taken from the HOLY BIBLE, NEW INTERNATIONAL VERSION®. Copyright © 1973, 1978, 1984 by International Bible Society. Used by permission of Zondervan Publishing House. All rights reserved.

ISBN 0-7644-9912-2
Printed in the United States of America.
10 9 8 7 6 5 4 3 2 1   00 99

CONTENTS

Welcome to Treasure Hunt Bible Adventure! 5

Your Contribution to
    Treasure Hunt Bible Adventure 6

The Overview 8

Gearing Up for the Adventure! 10

Jungle Gym Gems! 13

DAY 1 (The Bible shows us the way to trust.) 19

DAY 2 (The Bible shows us the way to love.) 27

DAY 3 (The Bible shows us the way to pray.) 34

DAY 4 (The Bible shows us the way to Jesus.) 42

DAY 5 (The Bible shows us the way to live.) 50

Welcome to TREASURE HUNT BIBLE ADVENTURE!

X marks the spot...for VBS excitement! Grab your compass, dust off your binoculars, and be sure your flashlight has batteries. You're hot on the trail to Treasure Hunt Bible Adventure, where kids discover Jesus—the greatest treasure of all! Your young adventurers will explore how the Bible maps the way to amazing riches, showing us the way to trust, love, pray, and live. Kids begin each day's treasure hunt by doing fun motions to new as well as familiar Bible songs during Treasure Hunt Sing & Play. Then they'll join with their Clue Crews to dig into Bible Exploration, create a wealth of treasures in Craft Cave, experience "vine" dining at Treasure Treats, view *Chadder's Treasure Hunt Adventure* video, and, of course, monkey around at Jungle Gym Games.

Jungle Gym Games is just one of seven Discovery Sites kids will visit each day of their Treasure Hunt Bible Adventure. At each Discovery Site, kids will experience the daily Bible Point in a new way. During their time at Jungle Gym Games, kids will play all-new games as they discover the treasure of knowing Jesus.

Leading Jungle Gym Games is easy and fun!

Kids of all ages will love playing these cooperative games with their Clue Crews. You'll enjoy your role and be most successful as a games leader if you

- enjoy playing games,
- like activity and are energetic,
- maintain a positive attitude,
- can organize and motivate children, and
- model God's love in everything you say and do.

Your Contribution

Your Contribution to TREASURE HUNT BIBLE ADVENTURE

Here's what's expected of you before, during, and after Group's Treasure Hunt Bible Adventure.

Before TREASURE HUNT BIBLE ADVENTURE

♣ Attend scheduled Discovery Site leader training.

♣ Pray for the kids who will attend your Treasure Hunt Bible Adventure.

♣ Ask your Treasure Hunt Director (otherwise known as your church's VBS director) what you should wear each day. Discovery Site Leader T-shirts (available from Group Publishing and your local Christian bookstore) help kids identify you—and help you identify other Discovery Site Leaders. If your Treasure Hunt Director doesn't order T-shirts, you may want to agree on another easily recognizable uniform such as tan shorts, an "explorer's" vest, and hiking boots.

♣ Read this Jungle Gym Games Leader Manual.

♣ Work with the Treasure Hunt Director to collect necessary supplies. You may want to list supplies in your church bulletin and ask church members to donate items such as balloons, a child's pool, towels, and plastic milk-jugs.

♣ Meet with the Treasure Treats Leader. You'll be helping the Treasure Treats Leader supervise each day's snack preparation, so you'll want to know the location of the kitchen and familiarize yourself with general Treasure Treats procedures.

♣ Meet with the Treasure Time Finale Leader. Each day's Treasure Time Finale will be a fun, involving review of the day's Bible story and will remind kids to carry out Operation Kid-to-Kid™! The Treasure Time Finale Leader will need all Discovery Site Leaders on hand to make things go smoothly. Be prepared to assist with distributing, displaying, or collecting props as needed.

During TREASURE HUNT BIBLE ADVENTURE

♣ Collect necessary supplies, and set up your playing area each day.

♣ Help the Treasure Hunt Sing & Play Leader demonstrate the motions to "I've Found Me a Treasure" on Day 1. You may have learned the motions in your

---

A CLUE FOR YOU!

It may be helpful to meet with the Treasure Hunt Director to go over the supply list. Let the director know what supplies you have or can collect on your own and what supplies you'll need to purchase or collect from church members. Open communication makes your job even easier!

leader training meeting.

♣ Welcome each new group of Clue Crews to Jungle Gym Games. You'll be leading three different groups each day.

♣ **NOTE:** *Each day except Day 1, the first group to report to you each day will do Treasure Treats Service instead of games. Meet your crews in the Treasure Treats area, and help the Treasure Treats Leader supervise crews as they prepare snacks for the entire VBS!*

♣ To help create a fun atmosphere and reinforce Bible learning, play the *Treasure Hunt Sing & Play* audiocassette or CD as kids play.

♣ Use your bamboo whistle or another attention-getting device to gather Clue Crews before you explain each game. This saves you from shouting and keeps kids from being distracted. Be sure everyone understands each game before you begin.

♣ Encourage and affirm each child; create an everybody-can-do-it environment. Be aware of kids with special needs, and find ways to help them succeed in the activities.

♣ Each day, Clue Crews will receive three clues for a Treasure Chest Quest. The Treasure Time Finale Leader is responsible for the Treasure Chest Quest and may ask you to distribute clues to the Clue Keepers in each Jungle Gym Games session.

♣ Repeat the daily Bible Point often. It's important to say the Bible Point just as it's written. Repeating the Bible Point again and again will help children remember it and apply it to their lives. Kids will be listening for the Point so they can shout, "Eureka!" Each day's games suggest ways to include the Bible Point.

♣ Attend and participate in each day's Treasure Time Finale.

After TREASURE HUNT BIBLE ADVENTURE

♣ Return, recycle, or throw away leftover supplies.

♣ Donate extra recreation items to your church, a preschool, a local community center, or a school.

♣ Remind kids of their experiences at VBS by
  ○ leading Jungle Gym Games at other children's ministry events,
  ○ phoning neighborhood kids who participated in Treasure Hunt Bible Adventure, and
  ○ sending Treasure Hunt Bible Adventure follow-up postcards.

A CLUE FOR YOU!

Attention-getting signals let kids know when it's time to stop what they're doing and look at you. You can use the bamboo whistle (available from Group Publishing or your local Christian bookstore) or another noisemaker of your choice. The first time students come to your Discovery Site, introduce and rehearse your attention-getting signal. Once kids are familiar with the signal, regaining their attention will become automatic.

Field Test Findings

Our Jungle Gym Games Leader started a trend when he had the kids say the Point and he jumped in the air and shouted "Eureka!" Not only did kids love it, but it gave them an opportunity to verbalize the daily Bible Point.

▼▼ TREASURE HUNT BIBLE ADVENTURE OVERVIEW ▼▼

This is what everyone else is doing! At Treasure Hunt Bible Adventure, the daily Bible Point is carefully integrated into each Discovery Site activity to reinforce Bible learning. Jungle Gym Games are an important part of kids' overall learning experience.

	BIBLE POINT	BIBLE STORY	BIBLE VERSE	TREASURE HUNT SING & PLAY	CRAFT CAVE	JUNGLE GYM GAMES
DAY 1	The Bible shows us the way to trust.	Peter walks to Jesus on the Sea of Galilee (Matthew 14:22-33).	"Do not let your hearts be troubled. Trust in God" (John 14:1a).	• He's Got the Whole World in His Hands • The B-I-B-L-E • Where Do I Go? • I've Found Me a Treasure (chorus and verse 1)	**Craft** Jungle Gel **Application** Kids need to trust the Craft Cave Leader that Jungle Gel really works. In the same way, we need to trust God when things in life seem impossible.	**Games** • Swamp Squish • Peter's Windy Walk • The River Bend • Treasure Tag • Pass-Along Peter **Application** The Bible teaches us that God is powerful and that we can trust him.
DAY 2	The Bible shows us the way to love.	Jesus washes the disciples' feet (John 13:1-17).	"A new command I give you: Love one another" (John 13:34a).	• Put a Little Love in Your Heart • I've Found Me a Treasure (add verse 2) • Jesus Loves Me	**Craft** Operation Kid-to-Kid Magnetic Bible Bookmarks **Application** Just as the magnet links the two children on the bookmark together, the Bible connects us with others around the world.	**Games** • Monkeys Love Bananas • Footrace • Gold Coin Keep-Away • Firefly Fling • Mosquito Net **Application** As the Bible shows us how to love, we can love others.
DAY 3	The Bible shows us the way to pray.	Jesus prays for his disciples and all believers, and then he is arrested (John 17:1–18:11).	"I pray also for those who will believe in me through their message, that all of them may be one" (John 17:20a-21b).	• Let Us Pray • Hey Now • I've Found Me a Treasure (add verse 3)	**Craft** Surprise Treasure Chests **Application** When kids open the treasure chest, they'll be surprised at the "riches" inside. When we open our hearts to God in prayer, we'll be surprised by his loving response.	**Games** • Savor the Flavor • Centipede Scurry • Message Mime • It's a Jungle! • Flowers of Blessing **Application** It's easy to talk to God.
DAY 4	The Bible shows us the way to Jesus.	Jesus is crucified, rises again, and appears to Mary Magdalene (John 19:1–20:18).	"For God so loved the world that he gave his one and only Son, that whoever believes in him shall not perish but have eternal life" (John 3:16).	• He's Alive • Make Your Home in My Heart • Good News • Oh, How I Love Jesus • I've Found Me a Treasure (add verse 4)	**Craft** Good News Treasure Pouches **Application** The colorful beads on the Treasure Pouch will remind kids of the good news that Jesus died for our sins and rose again!	**Games** • Roll Away the Stone • Butterfly Breakout • Manic Monarchs • Jungle-Bird Jiggle • He Has Risen! **Application** Our lives can be changed because Jesus rose from the dead.
DAY 5	The Bible shows us the way to live.	Paul stands firm in his faith, even in a shipwreck (Acts 27:1-44).	"If you love me, you will obey what I command" (John 14:15).	• The B-I-B-L-E • Got a Reason for Livin' Again • I've Found Me a Treasure (entire song)	**Craft** Rain Forest Creatures **Application** Kids add color and "life" to Rain Forest Creatures just as God's Word adds color and meaning to our lives.	**Games** • Man-Overboard Tag • Out to Sea • Snake Swap • Crash Course • Cargo Toss **Application** Even when life seems scary or difficult, we can have confidence that God is in control.

This chart maps out the entire program at a glance. Refer to the chart to see how your Discovery Site activities supplement other activities and help kids discover Jesus—the greatest treasure of all.

TREASURE TREATS	CHADDER'S TREASURE HUNT THEATER	BIBLE EXPLORATION	TREASURE TIME FINALE
Snack Peter's Adventure Cakes **Application** Peter's adventure began when he trusted Jesus. Jesus wants us to trust him, too.	**Video Segment** Chadder and his friends begin searching for a hidden treasure. They stumble onto the deck of the SS Hope, where Wally the parrot warns them to watch out for Riverboat Bob. Chadder's afraid, so Ryan, the first mate, tells him to trust God. The kids go to Whistle Cave, followed by Ned and Pete, two scraggly sailors who want the treasure for themselves. The kids find the treasure map, moments before they're trapped by a cave-in! **Application** • Where do you turn when you're afraid? • How does the Bible help you trust in God? • Mark your Student Book at a Trust Verse.	**Peter Walks on Water** • Experience being in a ship during a storm. • Try walking on "water." • Discuss how Peter learned to trust Jesus.	• Watch how a pin can go into a balloon, without popping the balloon! • Use balloons to review the story of Peter walking on the water. • Receive gem treasures as reminders that we are precious to God.
Snack Love Chests **Application** Jesus showed love for his disciples when he washed their feet. Today's snack shows that love is a great treasure.	**Video Segment** Chadder sits in an old mine car, and the car takes off, racing through the cave. Near the cave exit stands Riverboat Bob. He hits the hand brake and Chadder goes flying, right into the boxes Ryan has been stacking on deck. Chadder thinks Ryan will be mad, but Ryan says he follows Jesus' example of showing love. Chadder leaves to look for his friends, but runs into Riverboat Bob instead! **Application** • Role play how you think Ryan will react to the mess Chadder made. • How can the Bible help you when it's hard to love someone? • How can the Love Verse you highlighted help you love this week?	**Jesus Washes the Disciples' Feet** • Go on a barefoot hunt to find the Upper Room. • Have their feet washed by their Clue Crew Leader. • Help wash their Clue Crew Leader's feet. • Help one another put their shoes back on.	• See how someone shows unexpected love to the Treasure Time Finale Leader. • Receive heart locks and keys as treasures to remind them that loving actions open people's hearts.
Snack Prayer Treasure Mix **Application** Jesus' prayer teaches us to pray. The items in the Prayer Treasure Mix remind kids to pray about specific things.	**Video Segment** Chadder awakes in the mine and finds Hayley and Tim. They find a clue and decide to ask Ryan for help. The kids find Ryan in prayer, and Ryan shows them the Bible story of Jesus praying. Chadder wanders off, and Colonel Mike sees him and mistakes him for a scoundrel. Colonel Mike tells Chadder to walk the plank. **Application** • Pray in your crew for the child who'll receive your Spanish Bible. • Is there ever a time when you shouldn't pray? Explain. • How can you pray as Jesus taught?	**Jesus Prays** • Learn ways to pray for themselves. • Practice praying for various groups of people. • Create a mural with their hand prints to represent Jesus' prayer for all believers.	• Watch a skit about what it might be like for God to listen to our prayers. • Receive magnifying glass treasures as reminders that prayer brings us closer to God.
Snack Empty Tombs **Application** On the third day, Jesus' tomb stood empty. These scrumptious snacks are empty, too.	**Video Segment** Ryan explains that Chadder's a friend, and Colonel Mike points the kids toward the monkey tree. Chadder loses the map, but Ryan assures him that Jesus is the real treasure. The wind blows the map back again, and the hunt continues. The kids find the treasure chest, and Chadder finds the key to the chest hidden in the old tree. Just as they open the chest, Ned and Pete step up to steal the treasure. **Application** • How do you get to heaven? • How can knowing the treasure of Jesus change your life? • Why is it important to know about the treasure of Jesus?	**Mary Magdalene at the Empty Tomb** • Experience the sadness of the crucifixion. • Hear Mary tell how she searched for her lost treasure—Jesus—at the empty tomb. • Hear "Jesus" call their names; then draw crosses on their mural hand prints to thank God for Jesus.	• Pray; then give their sins to "Jesus" and watch as he makes the sins disappear. • Receive personal messages from their Clue Crew Leaders that Jesus loves them. • Receive three gold coin treasures as reminders that Jesus is the most valuable treasure we have.
Snack Sailboat Sandwiches **Application** When Paul faced a shipwreck, his trust in God helped him. We can live an adventurous life when we believe in God.	**Video Segment** Ned and Pete plan to take the treasure, but Riverboat Bob steps in to help. Bob reveals that he's been watching over the kids all along. Colonel Mike wants to throw Ned and Pete to the alligators, but Ryan convinces him to show God's love. Hayley, Tim, and Chadder fantasize about what they'll do with the treasure, but decide to give the money to Colonel Mike to help him bring supplies and Bibles to people along the river. **Application** • How can the Bible help you make decisions this week? • What do you think about giving your Spanish Bible away? Why? • When are times you can use the Bible verses you marked this week?	**Paul Is Shipwrecked** • Be "handcuffed," and led inside a prisoner's ship. • Hear a fellow prisoner tell about Paul's experience in the ship. • Experience a shipwreck. • Discuss how Paul's life was in God's control.	• Use a "chirping parrot" to experience the importance of working together to tell others about Jesus. • Present their Spanish translations of the Gospel of John as a special offering. • Receive a compass as a reminder that the Bible gives us direction in life.

9

Gearing Up for the Adventure!

GEARING UP FOR THE ADVENTURE!

A Clue for You!

If you have extra volunteers, you may want to try team teaching—a great way to facilitate larger groups. Set up and run two different games simultaneously; then blow your bamboo whistle, and have groups switch.

Jungle Gym Games Preparation

♣ Work with the Treasure Hunt Director to select an area for recreation. The games may be played inside or outside; in either case, you'll need a large, open playing area.

♣ Read each day's Jungle Gym Games. Choose activities that will work best with the game area you've chosen and with the number of Clue Crews you're expecting in each session.

♣ Photocopy the Jungle Gym Games sign and arrow on the inside of this manual's cover. Make as many arrows as you need to guide kids to your game area. Post the sign and arrows around your facility so kids can easily find the games area.

♣ Designate outside play areas with ropes or other markers—especially if you'll be playing in or near a parking lot.

♣ Consult with your Treasure Hunt Director to find out how many Clue Crews will be at Treasure Hunt Bible Adventure. You can expect one-fourth of the total number of Clue Crews to report for each Jungle Gym Games session. To lead games, you'll need one set of the following items. You can reuse the items for each session.

A Clue for You!

When rounding up supplies, remember that you'll only have one-fourth of the total number of elementary kids (and Clue Crews) at each session of Jungle Gym Games.

Things you can find around your home

- ○ strips of paper
- ○ empty plastic bowls (1 for each Clue Crew)
- ○ empty plastic milk jugs (1 for each child)

Gearing Up for the Adventure!

- ○ 1 children's wading pool
- ○ 2 laundry baskets
- ○ 2 or 3 large black trash bags
- ○ 1 watch with a second hand
- ○ 1 balloon pump or bicycle pump
- ○ bandannas or other strips of soft cloth
- ○ 1 yellow item to use as a banana
- ○ old towels

Things you can find around your church

- ○ masking tape or rope
- ○ 1 permanent marker
- ○ heavy tape (such as duct tape)
- ○ transparent tape
- ○ construction paper
- ○ scissors

Things to collect or buy

- ○ large sponge mitts (2 for each Clue Crew)
- ○ a variety of small candies
- ○ paper lunch sacks (1 for each Clue Crew)
- ○ 8- or 9-inch balloons of various colors
- ○ 2-60 balloons*
- ○ a bamboo whistle* or another attention-getting device
- ○ neon-colored tennis balls (1 for each Clue Crew)
- ○ Ping-Pong balls (1 for each Clue Crew)
- ○ drinking straws (1 for each child)
- ○ plastic tubing or an old garden hose
- ○ beach balls (1 for each Clue Crew)
- ○ 20 tennis balls of 2 different colors (10 tennis balls of each color)
- ○ plastic eggs (10 for each Clue Crew)

*Available from Group Publishing or your local Christian bookstore. Check your Treasure Hunt Bible Adventure catalog for a listing and description of these bright, durable items.

To Make Sure Your Jungle Isn't Too Wild...

♣ Have Clue Crew Leaders place their crews' treasure bags and any other personal items in a designated area, away from the playing area. Remind Clue Crew Leaders to collect their crews' items before they move to their next Discovery Site.

Field Test Findings

You'll use the balloon or bicycle pump to blow up several 2-60 balloons. (The name refers to the balloon size—two inches around and about sixty inches long.) Our Jungle Gym Games Leader discovered that you really do need a pump to inflate these skinny balloons! He almost passed out from trying to inflate them himself!

Look for a variety of small candies with easy-to-recognize flavors, such as cherry Life Savers, mints, caramels, chocolate kisses, and lemon drops. To make this game fun for everyone, don't use candies with *extremely* sour or bitter flavors.

A Clue For You!

Preschoolers will also be using Ping-Pong balls in one of their activities. Check with the Preschool Bible Treasure Land Leader to see if you can use the Ping-Pong balls too.

Gearing Up for the Adventure!

A Clue For You!

We have provided you with more games than you'll need to fill your time. Choose the games that best suit your children and your setting. Make Jungle Gym Games the best they can be for your Treasure Hunt Bible Adventure!

- - - - - - - -

♣ Choose a playing area that's large enough for everyone to move around freely. If you're playing outside, clear the area of sharp rocks or sticks that might injure children. If you're playing in a grassy area, you may want to provide insect repellent.

♣ Have the Materials Managers collect their Clue Crews' supplies immediately after each game.

♣ Remind children to tie their shoes before beginning an active game. If children are wearing sandals or other shoes that might slip, have them hop or take giant steps rather than run.

JUNGLE GYM GEMS!

A CLUE FOR YOU!

Kids of all ages love these Jungle Gym Gems. If you set up any of these centers, let your Preschool Bible Treasure Land Leader know about it. He or she may be able to let preschool adventurers explore these cool activities. Or see if the preschool leader would like to work with you on setting up several activities so elementary kids and preschoolers can share in the fun.

Add glitz to your games with these recreational riches! Set up one or more of these activity stations in your Jungle Gym Games area. Use these activity stations throughout the week in one or more of these ways:

♣ Use stations to fill time when one or two crews have arrived and you're waiting for others. Those who are early will have something fun to do and won't get bored standing around waiting. (Kids may even try to arrive early to take part in these "wowie" centers!)

♣ Have half the kids participate in games while the others use the activity stations; then switch so everyone gets to do both things.

♣ When it's almost time for kids to switch to a different Discovery Site and you don't have time to play a whole game, use these stations to give kids something to do for a few minutes.

♣ Due to the nature of the activity stations, only one crew can participate in each station at a time. Others can line up for a turn, or you can have several activity stations going at once. If your group is large, consider creating more than one of each activity station so children can participate more quickly.

♣ You can operate one station for the duration of your VBS, vary the stations daily, or rotate them throughout the week. In any case, these activities are so much fun that kids will want you to allow a little extra time for them to participate.

 Backward Waterfall

Supplies
- 1 children's wading pool (for best results, use a wading pool made of hard, shell-like plastic rather than an inflatable one)
- 1 large cinder block
- 1 Hula Hoop that will fit inside the wading pool
- Joy dish-washing liquid (this brand works best for this activity)
- light corn syrup
- water

Setup
- Pour 1 gallon of water, 5 cups of Joy dish-washing liquid, and 2 cups of light

Jungle Gym Gems!

Field Test Findings

This was so cool! The Backward Waterfall delighted kids of all ages—from tiny preschoolers to Crew Clue Leaders. They couldn't wait to try it!

Don't worry if the mixture doesn't work immediately. It works wonderfully after it's set for thirty minutes or more!

corn syrup into the wading pool. Stir gently until mixed.
- Place the cinder block in the center of the wading pool. If, after the block is in place, the bubble solution is less than two inches deep, mix another batch of bubble solution and add it to the pool. (You'll probably want to have another batch on hand anyway, as everyone will want a turn at this!)
- Place the Hula Hoop in the pool.

The Activity

Say: **When you're in the rain forest, you're likely to see a lot of beautiful waterfalls. We've got a new kind of waterfall here for you to experience...a backward waterfall!**

Have a child step directly onto the block and stand still with arms at sides. Ask another adult to help you grasp the Hula Hoop on both sides, and with a quick, smooth movement, lift the hoop straight up and above the child. This will create a huge bubble around the child, just like a waterfall going the wrong way!

After the bubble pops, have the child step out of the pool without stepping into the solution, and ask the next child to move onto the block. Repeat until everyone has had a turn.

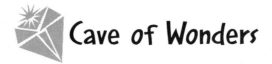

Cave of Wonders

Supplies
- 10 to 20 large boxes
- 1 utility knife
- duct tape or packing tape
- plastic "jewels" or rhinestones, coins, or rings
- glue

Setup
- Several weeks before your Treasure Hunt Bible Adventure begins, start collecting large packing boxes and appliance boxes. You'll need at least ten to twenty boxes; if you can add even more, the maze will be that much better.
- In a large room or outside, arrange the boxes in a maze configuration. Use your imagination, and turn boxes every which way! Be sure your maze includes a few T's or forks that force children to choose which way to go. You can also

A CLUE FOR YOU!
Although this treasure cave is fun anywhere, you may want to build excitement and mystery by placing it in a darkened, unused room. Mark the door with a sign that says "Cave of Wonders." Drape the doorway with black cloth or plastic, leaving a cutout for the cave entrance. Give each child a small flashlight to search out the wonders of the cave.

design "up and overs" by placing a low table (such as the kind preschoolers might use) in the middle of your maze. Stand a tall box on the floor at each end of the table, and then place boxes on the table as shown on pages 14 and 15.

● Once your maze is arranged, use a utility knife to cut a kid-sized doorway in each box. To create a doorway, cut three sides of a 2-by-2-foot square from one side of the box, leaving the bottom side of the square attached. Push the doorway cutout through the doorway of the connecting box to help "lock" the boxes together and create a path for kids to follow.

● After cutting all the doorways, use duct tape or packing tape to tape the boxes securely together.

● Glue a variety of plastic "jewels", coins, or rings on walls inside the maze. You might also want to make primitive drawings similar to those of ancient civilizations. For example, rough stick-figure drawings of people with a book might remind children to read the Bible. Or draw a funny Chadder picture on the walls. Maybe his ancestors lived long ago in these very jungles!

● Post "Cave Entrance" or "Treasure Seekers Only!" signs about the entrance of your maze. You might also want to decorate the outside with moss (green yarn or streamers), branches, or other reminders of the rain forest.

The Activity

Say: **Throughout the rain forests are caves that twist and turn into the sides of rocky mountains. Inside we might find treasures or other reminders of those who lived in these jungles before we came exploring. Let's see what we find!**

Allow only a few children to go through the maze at a time. (Too many kids may cause crowding and tearing of the maze.)

Afterward, ask children what they saw in the caves. Ask:

● **What treasures would you like to find in a cave?** (Diamonds; jewels; gold.)

● **What treasures do you think others find in you?** (My smile; my helpful attitude; my fun sense of humor.)

The *Real* Cave of Wonders!

Although the kids in your VBS may find colorful trinkets in this cave, you may want to tell them about a boy who *really* stumbled onto some amazing treasures in a cave. In 1947, a young Bedouin shepherd boy was searching for a lost goat in the hills near the Dead Sea. There he discovered a cave which held many mysterious clay jars. These jars contained leather and papyrus scrolls, dating back over one thousand years! The scrolls, which came to be known as the Dead Sea Scrolls, were copies of almost all of the Old Testament books, commentaries on Scripture, and notes about worship. These treasured scrolls have helped Bible scholars understand more about the Bible and verify its accuracy.

Treasure Dig

Supplies
- 1 children's wading pool (for best results, use a wading pool made of hard, shell-like plastic rather than an inflatable one)
- clean sand
- small paintbrushes
- small trinkets such as tiny plastic toys, bracelets, rings, or fake coins

Setup
- Pour several inches of sand into the wading pool. Place a variety of trinkets in this layer, pat them down, and then pour another couple of inches of sand on top. Place another layer of trinkets and sand, repeating the process until the sand is about two inches from the top of the pool.

1. This activity works best if the sand is a tiny bit damp. You don't want it to be wet, but if it's too dry, the activity creates a lot of dust. Try using a spray bottle to lightly mist each layer of sand.

2. This activity also works in an outdoors sandbox or a sandy playground area. Rope off an area with signs saying "Archaeological Dig," and bury trinkets in the area.

3. For a different spin on this idea, turn it into a paleontology dig. (This means you will be looking for fossils and old bones instead of the artifacts of past civilizations.)

Ask your local butcher for a variety of bones. Be sure to use large bones such as those in pork or beef ribs or bones a butcher would deem safe for a dog to gnaw. Chicken bones are not suitable.

Boil the bones until no meat remains on them; then wash them in a solution of bleach and water to be sure they're completely clean. Bury the bones as you would the trinkets. As children uncover the bones, help them imagine they're paleontologists trying to determine what kind of animal might have left these bones.

The Activity

Give several children small paintbrushes. Explain that you're treasure hunters, carefully digging for buried treasure. Say: **We might find treasures, or we might find artifacts or objects that tell us about people who lived in the rain forest long ago. Because treasures and old objects are delicate and could be damaged by rough treatment, archaeologists and others digging for treasure often use brushes to carefully remove the dirt.**

Show children how to make small sweeps in the sand with their little brushes. After a while, children will begin to find the treasures you've buried. Allow each child to find and keep one trinket; then have the child pass the brush to a waiting child.

Before a second group of children searches for treasure, stir the sand with your hands to bring more trinkets closer to the surface. If necessary, add more trinkets at this time as well.

While children are searching, ask:

● **What do we learn from what others have left behind?** (We learn how people lived in the past; we learn what life was like long ago.)

● **One hundred or one thousand years from now, what do you think people will find that we've left behind?** (Sports equipment; electronic games; books; computers.)

● **What do you think people will learn from what you leave behind?** Answers will vary.

● **How can we leave behind a message of God's love?** (Through things we write; by telling others what we know; people will pass stories about us on to children in the future.)

Field Test Findings

We allowed preschoolers to try this option, too. Although the trinkets were merely simple toys, the children were delighted that they got to keep a "treasure." This is a super way to incorporate the "delight factor" into your program!

Panning for Gold

Supplies

● 1 children's wading pool (for best results, use a wading pool made of hard, shell-like plastic rather than an inflatable one)
● clean sand
● small pebbles (such as those used in aquariums)
● gold spray paint
● newspaper
● aluminum pie plates
● 1 hammer
● 1 nail
● water
● candy or trinkets (optional)

Setup

● Spread a layer of small pebbles on newspaper, and spray-paint the pebbles

Field Test Findings

Our poor aluminum pie pans suffered the consequences of "gold fever"! In the excitement of searching for treasures, the kids scooped out mounds of sand, causing the inexpensive tins to crumple under the weight. In order to make your pie pans last, encourage kids to scoop a small amount of sand each time.

gold. When the paint is dry, turn the pebbles over, and paint the other sides as well. Repeat until you have a large supply of "gold nuggets."

● Pour about three inches of clean sand into the wading pool. Mix several handfuls of the gold nuggets into the sand. Pour water over this until the water is six to eight inches deep.

● Use a hammer and nail to make holes in the bottoms of the aluminum pie plates. Poke about ten or twelve holes in each plate so water and the finer bits of sand will sift through easily.

The Activity

Say: **When you're in the jungle, you often come across brooks, rivers, and pools of water, and you never know what you might find in them. Let's try our hand at panning for treasure!**

Give each child an aluminum pan. Demonstrate how to dip the pan into the sand and water and gently lift out a *small* amount of sand. Show children how to swirl the sand around in the pan until the water and sand have sifted out, leaving a gold nugget or two. Allow children to keep one gold nugget each, and return others they find to the pool. Then have children pass their pans to waiting children.

You can allow children to keep their gold nuggets, or you can give them the option of trading their gold for a treat such as a piece of candy or a trinket.

DAY 1

BIBLE POINT

The Bible shows us the way to trust.

BIBLE BASIS

Matthew 14:22-33. Peter walks to Jesus on the Sea of Galilee.

When Jesus called, "Come, follow me," Peter didn't hesitate to abandon his fishing nets in obedience. As Jesus' disciple, Peter listened to Jesus' teachings, watched Jesus heal the sick, and witnessed Jesus' power over wind and waves. He believed that Jesus was the Son of God. Perhaps that's why, on the stormy Sea of Galilee, when Jesus said, "Come," Peter ventured from the safety of a boat and walked toward Jesus. The water may have been cold, the waves may have been high, and the wind may have stung his face, but Peter knew that the safest place to be was with Jesus. When Peter became afraid and began to sink, "Immediately, Jesus reached out his hand and caught him." In the arms of Jesus, Peter learned to trust. He later wrote, "Cast all your anxiety on him because he cares for you" (1 Peter 5:7).

The disciple Peter is the perfect picture of our humanity and weakness; he reminds us how desperately we need Jesus. Children feel that need just as keenly as adults. They're familiar with the fear that accompanies life's "storms"—when parents divorce, friends move away, pets die, and classmates tease. The children at your VBS need to know that, in the midst of those hard times, Jesus is calling them to "come." And when children step out in faith, Jesus will be there with open arms, ready to catch them. Today's activities will encourage children to cast all their worries upon a loving, compassionate, and mighty God.

Day 1

Field Test Findings

In our field test, kids loved listening for the Bible Point so they could shout, "Eureka!" It almost became a Jungle Gym Game of its own!

🎯 BIBLE POINT

Jungle Gym Game Supplies

- ○ large sponge mitts (2 for each crew)
- ○ 1 children's wading pool
- ○ water
- ○ old towels
- ○ masking tape or a rope
- ○ 1 bamboo whistle or another attention-getting device
- ○ 8- or 9-inch balloons
- ○ plastic drinking straws (1 for each child)
- ○ construction paper
- ○ scissors

The Discovery Site

Before kids arrive, find out how many Clue Crews will visit Jungle Gym Games during each session. You can expect one-fourth of the total number of Clue Crews. For example, if your church has twenty Clue Crews, you'll be working with five crews (approximately twenty-five kids and five adult helpers) each session. As crews arrive, do a quick head count so you know the exact number of people in your group.

When all the crews have arrived, say: **Welcome to Jungle Gym Games! Each day when you visit this Discovery Site, we'll have fun playing new games that teach us more about the treasure we're discovering on our Treasure Hunt Bible Adventure. Today we're learning that 🎯 the Bible shows us the way to trust.** (Eureka!) Ask:

● **When is it hard for you to trust others? When is it hard for you to trust God?** (When things are hard; when I'm sad; when something seems impossible.)

● **How can you show that you trust others during Jungle Gym Games?** (By letting someone help me; by letting them do their best.)

Lead kids in one or more of the following Jungle Gym Games.

Day 1

JUNGLE GYM GAMES

Swamp Squish
(Energy level: High)

Field Test Findings

Brrr! The first kids to try this nearly froze their toes! Using warm water in the pool made the game more fun for everyone.

Supplies
- 2 large sponge mitts (the kind used to wash cars) for each crew
- 1 children's wading pool, with several inches of *warm* water in it
- 1 bamboo whistle or another attention-getting device
- a few old towels
- masking tape or a rope

Setup
- Mark a starting line for the relay using masking tape or a rope across the floor or ground.
- Place the wading pool at the far end of the playing area, opposite the starting line.

The Game
1. Have children remove their shoes and socks and place them to the side of the playing area so they remain dry.

2. Instruct each crew to line up at the starting line of the playing area. Ask Crew Leaders to count the members of their crews to determine if one or more children will need to run the relay twice (to make the teams even).

3. Give the first child in each line a pair of sponge-mitt "shoes," and demonstrate how these can be put on like socks.

4. Say: **In this relay, the first person in each crew must run to the pool, dip his or her feet into the water one at a time, run back, and pass the sponge shoes to the next person. Let's see how quickly we can all finish this relay.**

Be sure to demonstrate how to dip sponge-clad feet into the pool one at a time. If children run and jump into the pool with both feet at the same time, they are more likely to slip and fall. Insist on this safety measure.

5. Blow your whistle to signal "Go!"

6. When everyone has had a chance to race, gather the sponges. Say: **In today's Bible story, Peter walked on water to be near Jesus.** Ask:

A CLUE FOR YOU!

Sponge mitts are usually available in the car-maintenance section of stores. If you are unable to find any, sew two large sponges together on three sides to make a sponge "shoe" for this game.

A CLUE FOR YOU!

This game is best played outdoors, preferably in a grassy area where kids are less likely to slip.

Day 1

Field Test Findings

We discovered that sponge mitts soak up a lot of water! It was helpful to have someone stand near the pool to fill it up frequently.

● **How was this game like walking on water?** (There was water in the sponges; we got water all over our feet.)

● **Is this the same kind of walking on water that Jesus did in the Bible? Why or why not?** (No, Jesus was balanced on top of a lake of water; Jesus wasn't standing on the ground as we were.)

● **Why do you think Peter wanted to be near Jesus?** (Because he loved Jesus; because he was afraid.)

Say: **When Jesus walked on the water, it was a miracle. And when Peter walked out to Jesus on the water, that was a miracle too. Peter had to trust that Jesus would keep him from sinking. That's one way that ⊕ the Bible shows us the way to trust.** (Eureka!)

7. Provide children with towels to dry their feet if necessary; then have children put their shoes back on.

Peter's Windy Walk

(Energy level: Medium)

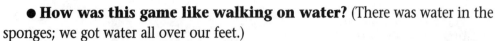

Larger balloons work best for this game, since they tend to stay aloft longer.

Supplies
● 8- or 9-inch balloons
● 1 bamboo whistle or another attention-getting device

Setup
● Inflate and tie off at least one balloon for each crew. Have a few extra balloons on hand in case some pop.

Although this game sounds simple, balloons and wind currents can be very uncooperative! Kids will realize that it takes gentleness, communication, and teamwork to keep the balloon under control.

The Game

1. Have each crew join another crew and form a circle. Give each group one balloon.

2. Say: **When Peter tried to walk on the water, there was a lot of wind. This game is a fun way to remember what it might have been like when Peter stepped out of the boat. We can pretend that our balloons are Peter and we are the wind and waves tossing him about while he tries to stay afloat.**

3. Tell children to stand close together in their circles; then toss the balloon up in the center, and show them how to gently blow upward to keep the balloon aloft. Blow your whistle to begin, and see which group can keep its balloon in the air the longest. Play as often as you like, watching groups improve their abilities as they learn to work together.

4. After a few minutes, gather the balloons and ask:

● **What kept your balloon from sinking to the ground?** (Our breath; blowing.)

● **What kept Peter from sinking when he tried to walk on the water?** (Jesus; God; God's power.)

Day 1

• **Why did Peter start to sink?** (He took his eyes off Jesus; he stopped trusting; he was afraid.)

• **What things make us doubt God?** (Hard times; when we're frustrated; when we're afraid; when things are scary.)

Say: **When we stopped blowing or let our blowing get out of control, our balloons fell to the ground. It's a good thing God is always in control of our lives.** ✪ **The Bible shows us the way to trust.** (Eureka!) **We can always trust God!**

The River Bend

(Energy level: Low)

Supplies
• masking tape or rope

Setup
• Use masking tape or rope to mark a large V on the ground. This will represent a river. The "river" should be very narrow at one end, then gradually widen until it's more than seven feet across.

The Game

1. Have children form pairs. This game will work best if partners are about the same size as each other. Gather children near the narrow end of the river.

2. Point to the river and say: **During our jungle treasure hunt, we've come to this river. You can't see them, but below the surface of this river, alligators and snakes are lurking. Since we don't want to fall into the river, we're going to have to make bridges.**

3. Have one pair of children join you at the narrowest point of the river. Tell these partners to face each other and clasp hands. Then have the partners walk along their respective banks of the river (the sides of the V). As the river widens, the children will have to move farther apart. As they move farther along the river, have them lean in and bear each other's weight. See how far they can progress before one or both of them fall into the river.

Repeat this with all the other pairs. Once one pair moves a few feet down the river, another pair can start so the game will move along at a quicker pace. If children would like to improve their distances, let them try again.

4. After everyone has had at least one turn, gather children and ask:

• **What was your strategy in this activity?** (I had to lean on my partner; we had to work together.)

• **Why was it important to trust your partner?** (If I hadn't trusted my partner, I wouldn't have gotten very far down the river; I had to trust my partner to keep from falling.)

• **What are ways we lean on God?** (By praying and asking for help; by

A CLUE FOR YOU!

If you expect to have more than twenty children at a time in your Discovery Site, make two or more rivers in order to move the game along more quickly.

A CLUE FOR YOU!

For extra excitement, choose a few volunteers to pretend to be alligators and snakes who kneel in the river. If a player steps or falls into the river, he or she may be tagged by an alligator or snake. Tagged players become alligators and snakes too!

Field Test Findings

Our games leader confessed that he was tempted to skip the debriefing questions for each game. But when he used them, he discovered that kids really *did* connect the activity to the Bible Point and story! *Games are actually one more way to reach kids who learn differently.*

Day 1

🏵 BIBLE POINT

reading the Bible to help us know what to do; by trusting God to take care of us.)

5. Say: 🏵 **The Bible shows us the way to trust.** (Eureka!) **This game demonstrates how important trust is! And trusting God is even more important than trusting a partner because God is really the only one who can save us.**

Treasure Tag

(Energy level: High)

Supplies
none

Setup
none

The Game

1. Form teams of three.

2. Say: **Choose one member of your team to be your team's Treasure. It might be easiest if you choose a smaller team member.**

3. When each team has chosen a Treasure, continue: **Everyone else on your team will form a Treasure Chest around the Treasure. You'll do this by holding hands around the Treasure. You'll remain in this formation throughout the game; don't let go of each other's hands.**

4. Select one team to be "It." Say: **This game is played just as regular Tag is played, with this exception: The Treasure who is "It" is the only one who can tag another Treasure. So it doesn't count if "It" tags a Treasure Chest player (someone on the outside ring). Or if a Treasure Chest player reaches through another circle to tag a Treasure, that doesn't count. The Treasure who is "It" must reach across his or her Treasure Chest, into another Treasure Chest, and tag the Treasure.**

5. Begin play. As soon as a Treasure is tagged, he or she becomes "It," and play continues. If the Treasure has trouble tagging others, ask another team to be Treasure Taggers as well.

6. After a few minutes, have groups gather. Ask:
● **What was it like to be a Treasure?** (Fun; hard; tiring; a little scary.)
● **What was it like to be a Treasure Chest?** (Hard, I had to keep watching; it was fun to protect the Treasure.)
● **Why did the Treasures have to trust their Treasure Chests?** (The Treasure Chests had to protect the Treasures; the Treasure Chests led the Treasures away from "It.")

Field Test Findings

Our Jungle Gym Games Leader was amused to find that the kids understood these instructions better than their Clue Crew Leaders! To make sure everyone understands, have two Clue Crew Leaders join hands to form a Treasure Chest around you. Have two kids form another Treasure Chest around a child. Demonstrate how to reach out from within your Treasure Chest and tag the other Treasure.

🏵 BIBLE POINT

Say: 🏵 **The Bible shows us the way to trust.** (Eureka!) **Just as the Treasures could trust the Treasure Chests, we can trust that Jesus will protect us. Jesus keeps us safe and surrounds us with love.**

Day 1

Pass-Along Peter

(Energy level: Low)

Supplies
- plastic drinking straws (1 for each child)
- construction paper
- scissors

Setup
- Use the template on page 26 to cut the figure of a man out of construction paper. You'll need one paper cutout for each crew.

The Game

1. Have kids gather in their crews and stand in a close circle.

Say: **When Peter was trying to walk on the water, he had to trust that Jesus would keep him from falling. We're going to play a game in which we pass Peter along and try to keep him from falling.**

2. Give each child a drinking straw, and give each crew one cutout. Demonstrate how to place the cutout in front of a straw and suck in, thus holding the paper at the end of the straw. Let kids try this so they understand how it works. Say: **We're going to see how long it takes to pass Peter from one straw to the next. If anyone in your crew drops Peter, pick him up and keep going.**

3. After each crew has passed the cutout around the circle, collect the cutouts, and throw away the straws. Say: **It's good that** ✪ **the Bible shows us the way to trust** (Eureka!) **because I don't think I'd trust being held up by your straws! Peter had to trust Jesus to help him, and that's what we have to do as well.**

Before kids leave, distribute any **TREASURE CHEST QUEST** Clues the Treasure Time Finale Leader has given you. When you hear your Treasure Hunt Director's signal, dismiss kids to their next Discovery Site.

Field Test Findings

It's a good idea to incorporate a low-energy game into each Jungle Gym Games session. In our field test, we discovered that kids (and Crew Leaders!) could use some "cool-down time" in their busy Treasure Hunt Bible Adventure day!

BIBLE POINT

TREASURE CHEST QUEST

PASS-ALONG PETER

DAY 2

BIBLE POINT

The Bible shows us the way to love.

BIBLE BASIS

John 13:1-17. Jesus washes the disciples' feet.

Jesus knew that his time on earth was coming to an end. His purpose would soon be accomplished, and he could return to heaven, to the side of the Father. Jesus' time with the disciples was coming to an end too. These followers, who gave up everything to follow Jesus and learn from him, must now carry his message to the world. What parting words would Jesus leave with them? How could he express his love for them and prepare them for the challenges ahead? Jesus' words were almost unnecessary, for his actions were unforgettable. The Son of God lowered himself to the position of a servant and washed his disciples' dusty feet. In this one simple act, Jesus demonstrated the depth of his love and modeled the servant's heart he desired in his followers.

It goes against human nature to put the needs of others ahead of our own. Our culture says to "look out for number one." We read magazines with titles such as Self and Moi. And we eat at restaurants where we can have it our way. Our world sends a self-centered and egocentric message to children, as well. That's why the children at your VBS can learn so much from Jesus' demonstration of love and humility. In today's activities, kids will experience the power of loving others through selfless acts. Children will discover that Jesus' actions are as unforgettable today as they were for the disciples nearly two thousand years ago.

Day 2

Field Test Findings

Although any yellow item will work, kids really loved using plastic bananas. Perhaps it added to the setting, or maybe they just thought it was silly!

Field Test Findings

Although it was easy to collect enough milk jugs for this game, a few of the milk jugs hadn't been rinsed out before they were donated. Yuck! We recommend preparing for this game a few days in advance so you can rinse all the milk jugs with a bleach solution…just in case!

Jungle Gym Games Supplies
- 1 yellow item to use as a banana
- at least 2 yellow beach balls
- empty plastic milk jugs (1 for each child)
- scissors
- neon-colored tennis balls (1 for each crew)
- rope or masking tape

The Discovery Site

Today kids will be learning about the love Jesus showed to his disciples and how they, too, can show love to others. The games planned for today reinforce the theme of God's love for us and our love for others.

After all the Clue Crews have arrived, gather kids and say: **Welcome back to Jungle Gym Games. What did you enjoy most yesterday during your Treasure Hunt Bible Adventure?** Allow a few kids to share their experiences. **Today we're learning that ✪ the Bible shows us the way to love.** (Eureka!) Ask:

● **How can you show love during Jungle Gym Games?** (By letting others go first; by calling out nice words; by cheering for others; by being gentle.)

● **What will our game time be like if everyone does those things?** (Fun; happy; exciting.)

Say: **Let's practice loving actions and words while we "monkey around" at Jungle Gym Games!**

Lead kids in one or more of the following Jungle Gym Games.

Day 2

JUNGLE GYM GAMES

Monkeys Love Bananas
(Energy level: High)

Supplies
● Any yellow item you can pretend is a banana. You might wrap a chalkboard eraser in yellow paper, use a yellow baton, or (if you're willing to risk the messy outcome) use a real banana! However, don't use a wooden item that might give splinters to children when they grab it.

Setup
none

The Game
1. Have children sit with their crews while you give instructions. Hold up the "banana" and say: **This is a banana, and after being out in the jungle, we all know monkeys love bananas. I'm going to assign each of you a monkey name. Say your monkey name aloud after I tell it to you. That'll help you remember what kind of a monkey you are!**

2. Assign each crew member one of the following monkey names:
- ● orangutan
- ● baboon
- ● chimpanzee
- ● spider monkey
- ● gorilla
- ● howler

Give the same names to the members of the other crews. This means in each crew there will be an orangutan, a chimpanzee, a gorilla, and so on.

3. Have kids form one large circle and sit down. Put the banana in the center of the circle.

Say: **When I call out a monkey name, listen to see if it's your kind of monkey. If I call your monkey name, run to the center of the circle, and try to snatch the banana before any of the other monkeys get it. For example, if I call "baboon" and you're a baboon, try to get the banana and get back to your seat in the circle before any of the other baboons gets the banana.**

4. Begin calling out monkey names from those you assigned. When a child successfully gets the banana and returns to his or her seat in the circle, give his or her crew (or team) a point. You can make things even more interesting by calling out two monkey names at once so more children are in the center trying to

If crews vary greatly in size, simply form groups of six for this game.

Day 2

A Clue for You!

This is a great time for Cheerleaders to do their stuff! Have Cheerleaders call out affirmations and encouragement as they lead their crew members in cheering for one another.

grab the banana.

5. When you've called all the monkey names at least once, let crews "go ape" and celebrate the points they've earned. Then ask:

● **We know monkeys love bananas. What foods do you love?** Answers will vary.

Say: **When we say we love food, what we really mean is we like that food a whole lot. Love is a lot stronger.** ✡ **The Bible shows us the way to love.** (Eureka!) **We show others we love them by our actions, just as Jesus showed love to his friends by washing their feet.**

Footrace
(Energy level: Medium)

Supplies
none

Setup
none

The Game

1. Have children remove their shoes and place them in a pile in the center of your playing area. Tell crews to sit at least ten feet from the shoe pile.

2. Say: **As we were trekking through the jungle on our treasure hunt, let's pretend we had to remove our shoes to cross a swamp. Now it's time to get them back on. Here's how: The person in your crew wearing the most green will be your crew's Runner.** Pause to let crews decide which person this will be.

Continue: **When I give the signal, the Runners will run up to the pile of shoes and begin holding up different ones. The rest of you may call out descriptions of your shoes or say yes and no to the shoes your Runner holds up. When a Runner gets a signal that he or she is holding up a pair of shoes belonging to someone in your crew, the Runner will quickly bring the shoes back to the crew and then go back to look for another pair. No one else from the crew may go to the shoe pile.**

When the Runner brings a pair of shoes to your crew, another crew member will put those shoes on the feet of their owner. You can't touch your own shoes, only the shoes of other crew members. And remember, someone has to put the Runner's shoes on for him or her, too!

3. When you're sure everyone understands the instructions, give the starting signal and begin the game.

4. When all shoes are on the correct feet, ask:

● **How did you feel about someone else finding your shoes and another person putting them on your feet for you?** (It was weird; I liked it; it made me feel strange.)

Field Test Findings

This turned out to be a neat team-building game. It provided an excellent opportunity for kids and leaders to serve each other in a fun way.

● **What did you think about putting your crewmates' shoes on for them?** (At first it was weird, but then it was OK; I didn't mind; I didn't like it.)

Say: **When Jesus washed the feet of his friends, they were embarrassed that he did this dirty job for them. But that was a way Jesus could show his friends how much he loved them.**  **The Bible shows us how to love.** (Eureka!) **When we help others, just as we helped one another in this game, we're showing them love.**

Gold Coin Keep-Away

(Energy level: High)

Supplies
● at least 2 yellow beach balls

Setup
none

The Game

1. Have kids form three teams. Instruct two of the teams to stand on opposite sides of the playing area. These are the Treasure Hunters. Have the third team stand in the middle. The members of this team are the Monkeys.

Say: **These beach balls are huge gold coins the Treasure Hunters have found. But they have to keep them away from the sneaky Monkeys, who want to keep the gold coins in the jungle.**

2. Give the balls to two of the Treasure Hunters to toss over the Monkeys to the other Treasure Hunters. Let the Treasure Hunters continue tossing or batting the balls until the Monkeys catch one of the balls. Whenever the Monkeys *do* catch a ball, have them switch places with either of the Treasure Hunter sides. This will give kids a chance to play both positions.

3. When all teams have had at least one turn being both Monkeys and Treasure Hunters, put away the balls and gather kids. Ask:

● **What do you have that you really love?** (My family; my bike; video games; my dog.)

A CLUE FOR YOU!

If you can't find yellow beach balls, use some of another color and have them represent jewels such as rubies, emeralds, or sapphires, depending upon the colors. In this way they can still represent precious treasures the monkeys are trying to steal.

Field Test Findings

We originally tried this game with one ball, but found that more kids got involved (and had more fun) when we used two or more "treasures."

Day 2

● **How do you treat that treasure?** (Carefully; I don't let others play with it; I put it away and take it out only on special occasions.)

● **How are we like a treasure to God?** (God loves us; God takes care of us; God wants what's best for us.)

BIBLE POINT

Say: ✲ **The Bible shows us the way to love.** (Eureka!) **From the Bible we know God loves us very much. We're a treasure to God! And even though it was fun to toss the gold coins around in this game, God would never treat us so carelessly. He loves us!**

Firefly Fling

(Energy level: Medium)

Supplies
- empty plastic milk jugs (1 for each child)
- neon-colored tennis balls (1 for each crew)
- scissors

A CLUE FOR YOU!

If a couple of kids in one or two crews seem to be hogging the ball, call out directions such as these every now and then:

● **Fling the firefly to the youngest person in your crew.**

● **Fling the firefly to your Clue Keeper** [or any other crew job].

● **Fling the firefly to the person with the longest hair in your crew.**

● **Fling the firefly to the person in your crew who is wearing the most purple** [or any other color].

● **Fling the firefly to the person in your crew who is wearing the most buttons.**

Setup
● Cut each milk jug around the middle about two inches below the handle. Discard the bottom half. The remaining half forms a plastic scoop in which children will catch balls. You'll need one scoop for each child.

The Game

1. Say: **There are a lot of fireflies at night out here in the jungle. They offer little bits of light in the dark jungle nights. That's kind of like kind and loving actions. They help bring light to our lives and the lives of others. In this game, as we fling fireflies around, we're going to fling around some ideas for loving others, too.**

2. Give each child a plastic scoop. Have children stay with their crews and form circles about the playing area. Give each crew one tennis ball.

3. Say: **These bright tennis balls are the fireflies. Use your scoop to toss them high into the air. Another crew member will catch the firefly in his or her scoop.** Demonstrate how this is done.

Say: **Before you toss a firefly up to light up the jungle sky, tell one way you can show love to others and add light to their lives. For example, you might say, "Give a hug" before you fling a firefly into the air.**

4. Begin the game. Encourage crew members to take turns throwing and catching the balls.

5. Gather all the scoops and balls, and say: **Just as** ✲ **the Bible shows us the way to love** (Eureka!)**, you've shown me today that you know a lot of ways to love. Try to see how many ways you can light up the lives of others around you with the actions you've mentioned today.**

Day 2

Mosquito Net
(Energy level: High)

Supplies
- rope or masking tape

Setup
- Use rope or masking tape to mark a section about six feet wide in the center of your playing area.

The Game

1. Say: **In the jungle there are so many mosquitoes that people often put a net called mosquito netting over their beds or other areas of their homes. In this game, some of you will be Mosquitoes, and some of you will be the Net that tries to catch the Mosquitoes.**

2. Select about one-fourth of your entire group to be the Net. Have these kids stand in the center of the area you've marked off in the playing area.

Say: **This area is the Net, and all the kids who are now in this area are part of the Net. All the rest of you are Mosquitoes. The Mosquitoes have to run back and forth through the Net. While you're in the Net area, the Net will be trying to tag you. If you're tagged, you stop being a Mosquito and become part of the Net and try to catch other Mosquitoes. The only place a Mosquito can't get tagged is outside of the Net area.**

3. Have all the Mosquitoes stand on one side of the Net; then have them all run through the Net at the same time. See how many get tagged and stay in the Net, becoming taggers themselves. Then have Mosquitoes run through the Net again and again. See how long it takes for everyone to become tangled in the Net.

4. When all Mosquitoes have been caught in the Net, gather kids and ask:

- **What happened when you got caught in the Net?** (I became part of the Net; I started tagging others.)

Say: **We can also get caught in nets in real life. When we hang out with people who like to do wrong things, it's easy for us to start doing wrong things, too. And when we hang out with friends who like to do good things and show love to others, it's easy to start doing good things and showing love.**

🎯 **The Bible shows us the way to love.** (Eureka!) **Jesus showed his friends love, and many of them then showed love to others. See if you can get your friends caught up in a net of love by doing good and loving things for them. They might get caught up and start doing the same thing!**

Before kids leave, distribute any **TREASURE CHEST QUEST** Clues you've been given. When you hear your Treasure Hunt Director's signal, dismiss kids to their next Discovery Site.

You'll need to modify the size of the playing area to accommodate the number of kids in each session. Keep the playing area narrow enough to prevent Mosquitoes from running too far around the Net.

🎯 **BIBLE POINT**

TREASURE CHEST QUEST

BIBLE POINT

✸ The Bible shows us the way to pray.

BIBLE BASIS

John 17:1–18:11. Jesus prays for his disciples and all believers, and then he is arrested.

We can only imagine the power and peace Jesus drew from his times in prayer. How he must have relished those all-too-brief moments—talking with the Father, pouring out his heart, praying for those he loved, and praising God. Perhaps that's why Jesus so often prayed privately, slipping away from the crowds to spend a few intimate hours with the heavenly Father. But this time was different. After the Passover meal, Jesus prayed, allowing his disciples to hear the burdens of his heart. And although the pain and suffering of the Cross were only hours away, Jesus prayed for his disciples and those they would lead. With his eyes turned toward heaven, Jesus spoke words of love and concern, words of finality and unity. In an intimate moment with the Father, Jesus spoke of those he loved and cared for…including you and me.

Although prayer is a key element in a child's relationship with God, praying can be difficult for children to understand or practice. Since they can't see God, children may feel confused about talking with God or disconnected when they try. That's why the kids at your VBS will appreciate today's activities. They'll learn that God really *does* hear our prayers, that we can use simple words when we pray, and that Jesus loved us so much that he prayed for us. Children will experience meaningful and creative prayers to help them discover the joy of spending time with God.

Day 3

Jungle Gym Games Supplies

- a variety of small candies
- paper lunch sacks
- masking tape or rope
- strips of paper
- 8- or 9-inch balloons in various bright colors
- 1 permanent marker
- 1 bamboo whistle or another attention-getting device
- *Treasure Hunt Sing & Play* audiocassette (optional)
- audiocassette player (optional)

Remember to give kids an opportunity to verbalize the Point while *you* respond with a resounding "Eureka!"

BIBLE POINT

The Discovery Site

Today's games focus on ways to communicate various messages as children learn about communicating with God through prayer. When children arrive, ask:

● **What's been the greatest thing about Treasure Hunt Bible Adventure so far?** Answers will vary.

Say: **Today we're learning that ✪ the Bible shows us the way to pray.** (Eureka!) **Prayer is important because it's how we communicate with God. In Jungle Gym Games, we'll discover that prayer can be fun and exciting. So let's get moving!**

Savor the Flavor

(Energy level: Low)

Supplies

● a variety of small candies with easy-to-recognize flavors, such as cherry Life Savers, mints, caramels, chocolate kisses, and lemon drops. Don't use candies with *extremely* sour or bitter flavors, as you want this game to be fun for everyone.

● paper lunch sacks

Day 3

Setup

● Unwrap the candies, and put an assortment into each paper sack. Make each bag of flavors unique so that crews can't guess flavors based on what they've overheard other crews say. You might want to include several candies of some flavors in a bag and not include one flavor in another bag. Just be sure to put five candies in each bag. You'll need one bag for each crew.

The Game

1. Have crews line up with all members facing the same direction. (Everyone should be facing the back of the person in front of him or her.) Instruct crew leaders to stand at the end of their lines; then give each crew leader one bag of assorted candies.

2. Tell the person standing next to the crew leader in each line to close his or her eyes, turn, and face the crew leader. This means that everyone in the line will be facing forward except the person next to the crew leader.

Say: **When I give the signal to begin, each crew leader will reach into his or her bag, pull out a piece of candy, and put it into the mouth of the crew member standing next to him or her. That person may open his or her eyes only after the candy is all the way into his or her mouth. No peeking!**

When you have a candy in your mouth, suck or chew on it until you recognize the flavor. Then quickly turn and whisper the flavor into the ear of the next crew member. Crew members will continue to whisper the flavor on down the line until the message reaches the first person. He or she will then run to the end of the line and tell your crew leader what the flavor is. If it's correct, then that person will stay, close his or her eyes, and get the next piece of candy. If the guess isn't correct, the first person will return to the front of the line until the correct message is passed. We'll continue until the sacks are empty.

Just a caution: If kids on another team hear your whispers, they might try guessing the same thing on their turns, so be sure to whisper quietly!

3. Begin play. Be sure crew members who are waiting to hear the message remain facing away from the crew member tasting the candy. This will prevent them from seeing the candy and getting ahead in the game. When each crew has gone through all its candies, have kids form one big circle and sit down.

4. Ask:

● **What was tricky about this game?** (Guessing the correct flavor; trying to understand other crew members, especially if they had candy in their mouths!)

● **What happened if the message got mixed up along the way?** (It slowed us down; we had to try again.)

Say: **When we pray, we're sending messages to God—messages of thankfulness, love, or need.** Ask:

● **What's it like to know that God always gets your messages?** (Great; a relief; it makes me feel glad.)

Field Test Findings

Some of our staff thought kids might fib about the candy flavor in order to get more candy. But kids got so caught up in accomplishing their task, they didn't have time to be greedy!

Field Test Findings

This was a wonderfully quiet game. Kids were so focused on tasting the candy and passing the message along, you would never have known you were in a room with more than twenty-five children!

Say: ✺ **The Bible shows us the way to pray.** (Eureka!) **You can be sure that God always hears our message correctly.**

✺ **BIBLE POINT**

Centipede Scurry

(Energy level: High)

Supplies
- masking tape or rope

Setup
- Use the masking tape or rope to mark a starting line and a finish line.

The Game

1. Say: **In the jungle are all kinds of creepy, crawly creatures such as centipedes. We're going to become centipedes with a mission. The mission is to get "home" first to let our centipede mothers know a centipede-eating bird is headed our way. You've got to move quickly, or you'll get gobbled up!**

2. Have each crew line up behind the starting line and place their hands on the hips of the person in front of them. In this way, each crew forms a centipede. Point out the centipedes' home (the finish line).

Have one crew move out in front to help you demonstrate how the centipedes will move. The centipede takes three giant steps then stops. The first person in line runs around the centipede twice and then stands at the end of the line, and the centipede takes three more giant steps. The person now at the head of the line then runs around the centipede twice, and the pattern is repeated. Explain that the goal is to see how quickly each centipede can get home.

3. When everyone understands how the centipedes will move, have your demonstration crew return to the starting line. Begin the race. As crews slowly progress across the playing area, they may realize that the closer they squish together, the faster their crewmates can run around them.

4. When all of the centipedes have made it home, gather everyone and ask:

- **Have you ever needed to give someone an important message? Explain.** Allow several kids to share.

Say: **Some messages are urgent, and other messages are just important. For example, it's important to tell people that we love them and that they're special.** Ask:

- **What are some important things to tell God?** (How much we love God; how great God is; we should say thank you to God.)

Say: **It's a good thing that ✺ the Bible shows us the way to pray.** (Eureka!) **We know that when we need to get a message to God, all we have to do is say it! God can always hear the message we're trying to give him.**

✺ **BIBLE POINT**

Day 3

Message Mime

(Energy level: Medium)

Supplies
none

Setup
● If playing indoors, there is no setup. If playing outdoors, use ropes as lines for kids to run across on opposite sides of the playing area.

The Game

1. Form two teams—Team A and Team B—and have teams line up facing each other in the center of the playing area. There should be about four feet of open space between the teams.

2. Say: **In this game, each team will take a turn acting out a message for the other team. You'll have to act out a message using no words, only actions and hand motions. We'll have Team A act out a message first. But first, I'll explain how the game works.**

Both teams will stand in the middle of the playing area, facing each other just as you are now. Team A will begin acting out its message while Team B calls out guesses. As soon as anyone on Team A hears anyone on Team B call out the correct message, he or she should turn and run toward "home." (If you're playing indoors, a player reaches home by touching the wall behind his or her team. If playing outdoors, a player reaches home by running across the rope line behind his or her team.) **When you see your teammate running for home, run with them!**

Team B, when you see members of Team A starting to run for home, start chasing them. If you tag any of them before they reach home, they join your team. Then we'll line up again and let Team B have a turn at acting.

3. Have members of Team A huddle together out of earshot of Team B and choose a message. Suggest words having to do with Treasure Hunt Bible Adventure, such as "treasure hunt," "eureka," "rain forest," "Chadder," and "Bible." If kids would rather act out names of favorite cartoons, foods, or other things, that's OK as well, as long as their choices are not offensive or in poor taste.

4. When the members of Team A are ready, have them line up in the center of the playing area, facing Team B, with about four feet of open space between them. Call out: **Action!** and let Team A begin acting out its message. After Team B correctly guesses the message and chases Team A home, have those children who were tagged join Team B. Now have Team B huddle and decide on a message to act out. Repeat the game as often as you like, with the team sizes changing after each round as kids are tagged and switch sides.

5. Gather kids and ask:

● **What was hard about acting out your message?** (I didn't know how to act out certain words or sounds; I was thinking about their guesses so I'd know when to run.)

● **What was hard about trying to guess the message?** (Trying to figure out the motions; I was laughing too hard!)

● **What if we had to act out all our messages to God? What would that be like?** (I'd never pray! It would be too hard; I don't think God would know what I was saying.)

Say: **I'm glad that ✪ the Bible shows us the way to pray.** (Eureka!) **We know that whenever we talk to God, our message is heard loud and clear!**

✪ **BIBLE POINT**

It's a Jungle!

(Energy level: Low)

Supplies
● strips of paper

Setup
● On each slip of paper, write the name of a jungle animal. Write the same name on five slips of paper; then list another animal five times and so on. You'll need one slip of paper for each child. Choose creatures that make distinctive sounds or motions that children can easily imitate. Here are some examples:

- ● monkey
- ● bird
- ● elephant
- ● lion
- ● snake
- ● mosquito
- ● hyena

The Game

1. Say: **In this game we're going to pretend it's a jungle in here** ["out here" if you're outside]. **I'm going to pass out slips of paper with the names of animals written on them. Don't let anyone see your paper unless you can't read yet. If you can't read your paper, ask a crew leader to whisper to you what's written on it.**

2. Pass out the papers, reminding kids to keep the words a secret. When each child has a paper, say: **There are a few other kids in the jungle who are**

Day 3

the same animal or creature as you. You've got to find them quickly! But instead of calling out the name of your creature, you've got to pretend you're that creature and make motions or sounds it might make. While you're acting like an animal, look for others who are doing the same thing you are, and join them. Let's see how quickly all you animals can find your friends.

3. Begin the game, and encourage kids to continue their noises and motions until they've all found their animal groups. Then have kids sit in their animal groups, collect the slips of paper, and ask:

● **What animals do we have here?** (Let each group identify itself by name and demonstrate how the animal sounds or acts.)

● **How do animals give messages to each other?** (Hoots; thumps; screams; growls.)

● **How do we give messages to each other?** (By talking; by whispering; by our actions.)

● **How do we give messages to God?** (By talking to God; by our actions; by singing.)

❂ BIBLE POINT

Say: ❂ **The Bible shows us the way to pray.** (Eureka!) **Jesus gave us a good example of how to talk to God. We know from the Bible that God always understands what we're telling him when we pray.**

Flowers of Blessing

(Energy level: Medium)

Supplies

- 8- or 9-inch balloons in various bright colors
- 1 permanent marker
- 1 bamboo whistle or another attention-getting device
- *Treasure Hunt Sing & Play* audiocassette (optional)
- audiocassette player (optional)

Setup

● Inflate the balloons. You'll need at least one balloon for every child, but it's a good idea to have extras in case a few pop.

● Use a permanent marker to write one of the following words on each balloon:

● friend   ● family   ● teacher   ● neighbor

The Game

1. Say: **In the jungles of the rain forest, there are beautiful flowers in a wide variety of bright colors. We're going to pretend these balloons are flowers floating about us. When I blow the whistle, start tossing balloons into the air. Let's see if we can get all the balloon**

flowers up in the air at once! When I blow the bamboo whistle again, grab a balloon, and sit down as quickly as you can.

2. Blow the bamboo whistle to signal kids to begin tossing the balloons into the air. After a minute, blow the whistle again, and wait until each child has grabbed a balloon and has sat down.

3. Say: **Look at the word written on your balloon. Since today we're learning that** ✲ **the Bible shows us the way to pray** (Eureka!), **we're going to take a few seconds from our game to pray. Pray for someone, using the word on your balloon as a guide. If it says "friend," you can pray for any one of your friends. If it says "family," you can pray for one person in your family and so on.**

Have children stop talking and quietly bow their heads for about fifteen seconds of prayer. Then blow the bamboo whistle, and have kids toss the balloons in the air. After about a minute, blow the whistle again, and have kids repeat the prayer activity.

4. Repeat the activity three or four more times; then collect the balloons, and ask children to bow their heads as you pray: **Lord, we thank you that we can talk to you any time about anything. Thank you for hearing our prayers. We're glad you gave us the Bible to show us the way to pray. Amen.**

Before kids leave, distribute any **TREASURE CHEST QUEST** Clues you've been given. When you hear your Treasure Hunt Director's signal, dismiss kids to their next Discovery Site.

This is a fun time to play the *Treasure Hunt Sing & Play* audiocassette or CD. While kids are tossing balloons in the air, play upbeat songs such as "Let Us Pray" or "Put a Little Love in Your Heart." Turn off the music when you want kids to grab a balloon and sit down.

TREASURE CHEST QUEST

BIBLE POINT
❃ The Bible shows us the way to Jesus.

BIBLE BASIS
John 19:1–20:18. Jesus is crucified, rises again, and appears to Mary Magdalene.

Jesus' crucifixion was both a devastating and defining event for his followers. Although Peter, a close friend and disciple, denied knowing Jesus, Joseph of Arimathea and Nicodemus, who had been secret followers, came forward in their faith to bury Jesus. Even Mary Magdalene thought she'd lost her greatest treasure. Seeing the empty tomb, Mary probably assumed someone had stolen Jesus' body. Through her tears, she told the angels, "They have taken my Lord away, and I don't know where they have put him." Jesus, her treasure, was gone, and more than anything Mary wanted to find him. Mary didn't need to search for long. Jesus lovingly called her name, revealing himself and the miracle of his resurrection.

The greatest treasure children can find is Jesus. For in knowing Jesus, children will experience forgiveness, love, and eternal life. However, like Mary, the kids at your VBS may have trouble "seeing" Jesus. Mixed messages from the media, school, and non-Christian friends may confuse kids or mislead them. But just as Jesus called Mary by name, Jesus calls each of us by name, too. He knows the hearts and minds of the children at your VBS. Today's activities will help children discover that Jesus is the greatest treasure of all, and that he's right there, waiting for them with open arms.

Day 4

Jungle Gym Game Supplies

- ○ large black trash bags
- ○ balloons
- ○ transparent tape
- ○ masking tape or rope
- ○ 1 watch with a second hand
- ○ 2-60 balloons
- ○ 1 balloon pump or bicycle pump
- ○ 1 bamboo whistle or another attention-getting device
- ○ bandannas or other strips of soft cloth
- ○ a large supply of plastic eggs

The Discovery Site

Today's games remind children of the excitement surrounding Jesus' resurrection and help them understand that their lives can be changed because of this.

Kids love the butterfly balloons used in Butterfly Breakout. If you have time to twist enough balloons, send one home with each child as a reminder of the change that happens in our hearts when we have a relationship with Jesus.

Plastic eggs are easy to collect from church members. Either add your request to a church bulletin, or make an announcement at the end of Treasure Time Finale on Day 1. Soon you'll be up to your legs in eggs!

Roll Away the Stone

(Energy level: Medium)

Supplies

- large black trash bags
- balloons
- transparent tape
- masking tape or rope

Setup

- Inflate the balloons, and fill the black trash bags with them. When a bag is

Day 4

A Clue For You!

Let the number of children at the Discovery Site determine the size of your playing area. Half the children will be using their bodies to block the other children, so if the playing area is too large, children will simply run around the Guards and the game won't be challenging.

A Clue For You!

If your group has more than forty children in it, form two smaller playing areas, and have two games of Roll Away the Stone going at the same time.

---

full of balloons, tape the top of the bag closed, thus forming a huge, lightweight "stone." You'll need only one stone, but you may want to create a few extras in case kids get carried away and pop one of them.

● Use the masking tape or rope to create a starting line and a finish line on opposite sides of the playing area.

The Game

1. Say: **After Jesus' friends placed his body in the tomb, soldiers rolled a huge, heavy stone in front of the opening to keep people out. Then guards came and stood in front of the tomb. They wanted to be sure no one got into that tomb.**

The Bible tells us that after three days, an angel of God came, and the heavy stone was rolled away. The guards were so afraid of the angel that they fainted. And when people looked inside the tomb, Jesus wasn't there! He had risen from the dead!

In this game we're going to pretend to be the guards and angels on that morning.

2. Form two teams: the Angels and the Guards. Have the Guards spread out within the playing area. Say: **Once you've decided where to stand, plant your feet there. Guards can wave their arms, but they cannot move their feet.**

3. Have the Angels line up at the starting line. Give the trash-bag stone to one of the Angels. Say: **This is the stone you must roll away. Your goal is to roll the stone away from this line all the way to the finish line as quickly as you can. Here are the rules:**

First, Angels may only roll or push the stone. They can't throw it into the air.

Second, the Angel with the stone can take only five steps; then the stone must be passed to another Angel. An Angel can't touch the stone again until at least two other Angels have had a turn pushing it.

Third, the Guards can block the stone with their arms and can even bat it up into the air back toward the starting line. But Guards must remember not to move their feet.

4. When everyone is ready, signal "go" and begin timing. See how long it takes the Angels to get the stone to the finish line. When they've done this, announce their time.

5. Switch teams so the Angels become the Guards and vice versa. Play the game again, and determine which team is fastest in moving the stone to the finish line. If time permits, play the game again to allow both teams to try to improve their original times.

6. Gather kids and ask:

● **In today's Bible story, why do you think the angels moved the stone?** (So everyone could see that Jesus was alive; to help people see that Jesus wasn't there.)

● **How can you "see" Jesus today?** (When I read the Bible; when people are kind; when I hear people talk about God.)

Say: 🌸 **The Bible shows us the way to Jesus.** (Eureka!) **He's our greatest treasure! The angels wanted the world to know that nothing—not even death—was strong enough to hurt Jesus. Now we can celebrate because Jesus' life gives us new life, too!**

Butterfly Breakout

(Energy level: High)

Supplies
- 2-60 balloons (these are the long, skinny balloons used to create balloon animals)
- 1 balloon pump or bicycle pump
- masking tape or rope
- 1 watch with a second hand
- 1 bamboo whistle or another attention-getting device

Setup
- Use a pump to inflate the balloons. Fill the balloons, but don't over-inflate them.

Tie the two ends of a 2-60 balloon together to create a circle. Hold the knot in one hand and the opposite side of the balloon in the other hand. Bring these together, and twist to create a figure-eight. This creates a simple butterfly.

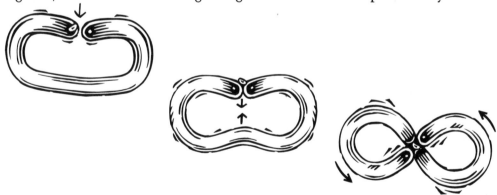

You'll need one butterfly for every crew. Make a few extra in case a few pop.
- Use the masking tape or rope to mark a starting line.

The Game

1. Say: **You might see beautiful butterflies in the jungle. After butterflies come out of their cocoons, they fly away. This is a race to see how far away from the cocoon your butterfly can fly.**

2. Have crews line up behind the starting line. Say: **Right now you're in your cocoon.**

🌸 **BIBLE POINT**

A CLUE FOR YOU!

The term 2-60 means that, when the balloons are inflated, they're about two inches around by sixty inches long. There are other dimensions for narrower balloons and ones of different lengths.

Day 4

Day 4

Field Test Findings

Although this game is similar to Centipede Scurry (played on Day 3), kids enjoyed using the balloons. Also, in a busy Treasure Hunt Adventure day, it's nice to play a game that's a little familiar!

Ask one crew to move out in front of the others to help you demonstrate the game.

Say: **The person at the end of the line will hold the butterfly and pass it over his or her head to the next person. As soon as the butterfly is passed, the last person in line will run to the front of the line. This way, the butterfly is continually passed overhead toward the front of the line, just as if it's flying!**

The second the butterfly leaves your hands, you can run to the front of the line. Your line doesn't have to be squished together; you might get farther if you spread out a little as you go, but remember that the butterfly can't touch the floor, so don't move too far apart.

If your butterfly touches the ground, everyone in your crew must freeze and count to ten as fast as you can. Then pick up the butterfly, and get it flying again!

I'll time you all to see how far you can go in one minute. When you hear the whistle, freeze!

3. When everyone understands the instructions, have all crews stand behind the starting line (in the cocoon), give a butterfly balloon to the last crew member in each line, and begin timing. After one minute, blow your whistle and see which team has gotten its butterfly the farthest from the cocoon.

4. If time permits, play the game again to see if teams can improve their technique and speed. Then collect the butterfly balloons, gather everyone, and say: **When a butterfly breaks out of its cocoon, it will never return to it. The cocoon can't hold the beautiful butterfly any longer.** Ask:

● **How can a butterfly remind us of Jesus?** (Jesus left an empty tomb behind, and a butterfly leaves an empty cocoon behind.)

✸ BIBLE POINT

Say: **The grave couldn't hold Jesus any longer. He has risen from the dead and will never die again.** ✸ **The Bible shows us the way to Jesus** (Eureka!)**, and when we know Jesus, we can have new life too.**

Manic Monarchs

(Energy level: High)

Supplies

- bandannas or other strips of soft cloth for tying legs together
- masking tape or rope
- 1 bamboo whistle or another attention-getting device

Setup

- Use masking tape or rope to mark start and finish lines about twenty feet apart.

Day 4

The Game

1. Have kids form pairs. Say: **As you know, there are often a lot of butterflies in the jungle. I want you and your partner to turn yourselves into butterflies right now!**

Give each pair a bandanna or strip of soft cloth, and have pairs loosely tie two of their legs together as for a three-legged race. Explain that their outside arms and legs are the upper and lower wings of the butterfly while their torsos and middle legs are the body of the butterfly.

2. Have butterflies line up behind the starting line. Say: **When I blow the whistle, start running and flapping your wings like a butterfly. We'll see how fast your butterflies can cross the finish line.**

3. Begin the game. When everyone has crossed the finish line, encourage kids to applaud each other (by clapping their wings together, of course!). Then allow kids to run the race again if time allows.

4. Have children remove the ties from their legs and hand them to you. Then have everyone sit together. Ask:

● **We can pretend we're butterflies, but when we ask Jesus into our lives, how are we like real butterflies?** (We change into new people just as a caterpillar changes into a butterfly; we'll never be the same.)

● **How is your life different when you follow Jesus?** (He forgives my sins; I know I'll go to heaven; I want others to know about him.)

Say: ✺ **The Bible shows us the way to Jesus.** (Eureka!) **Because Jesus died and rose again, we can believe in him and be changed. Just as a caterpillar changes into a beautiful butterfly, Jesus changes our lives. And just as a butterfly never goes back to being a caterpillar, we are forever changed by Jesus.**

✺ **BIBLE POINT**

Jungle-Bird Jiggle

(Energy level: Low)

Supplies

● a large supply of plastic eggs (the kind used at Easter)

Setup

none

The Game

1. Have children sit together in their crews.

Say: **In the jungle there are thousands of colorful birds. Let's pretend you're some of these colorful birds and you're trying to lay your colorful eggs in a tree. First, choose one person on your team to be your Tree. Everyone else will be Birds.**

When each crew has chosen a Tree, have Trees stand up beside their crews and

Day 4

Field Test Findings

This activity is a challenge, but kids enjoyed tackling it! We were amazed by their creativity and by how well they worked together to attempt such a feat!

🟢 **BIBLE POINT**

strike a "tree-like" pose. Have Trees stay frozen in these positions.

2. Distribute ten plastic eggs to each crew. Say: **When I say "go," all the Birds must lay their eggs by balancing them anywhere on the Tree. Work together, and as soon as you've balanced all ten eggs, sit down around your Tree and start to crow loudly so everyone will know you've finished.**

3. Begin the egg laying! This task is very difficult. If any crew manages to balance all its eggs long enough to sit and crow about it, congratulate the crew. If, after several minutes, no crew has been able to balance the eggs on its Tree, call time, gather the eggs, and have everyone sit down.

4. Ask:

● **What was hard about this game?** (Trying to balance so many eggs; the Tree kept moving, and our eggs kept falling.)

● **What things in life seem impossible or hard?** (Math; getting along with my family; saving my allowance to buy new toys.)

Say: **Succeeding in this game was nearly impossible! And sometimes life can seem hard or impossible. But you know what? Jesus came back to life after being dead, and most people would say that's impossible!** Hold up a plastic egg and split it open. **Just as these eggs are empty, Jesus' tomb was empty because he came back to life. Nothing is impossible for Jesus!**

Our Bibles show us more seemingly impossible things that Jesus did. 🟢 **The Bible shows us the way to Jesus.** (Eureka!)

He Has Risen!

(Energy level: Medium)

Supplies
● bandannas or other soft strips of cloth to use as blindfolds (1 per child)

Setup
none

The Game

1. Say: **When Jesus' friends first discovered that his tomb was empty, an angel at the tomb told them, "He has risen!" and instructed them to go tell others what had happened.**

Now, on Easter, many Christians greet each other by saying, "He has risen!" and the other person answers, "He has risen indeed!" This game is a fun way of reminding us of what the angel told those friends of Jesus long ago.

2. Choose one person to be "It," and give everyone else blindfolds. Have children wait to put on their blindfolds until you've given complete instructions.

Day 4

Say: **After you have your blindfolds on, slowly walk around the playing area. When you bump into someone, say, "Jesus has risen!"** If that person answers, "Jesus has risen!" then just continue to slowly mill about until you bump into another person. However, if you bump into someone and say, "Jesus has risen!" and that person answers, "He has risen indeed!" that means you've bumped into [name of child who is "It"]. **Join elbows with this person. Now if anyone bumps into either of you, you should answer, "He has risen indeed!" Then that person will link elbows with you and join in saying, "He has risen indeed!" We'll see how long it takes for everyone to know that Jesus has risen indeed!**

3. Have crew leaders help younger children secure their blindfolds so there's no peeking; then begin the game. When everyone has joined the line saying "He has risen indeed!" let children remove their blindfolds. Collect the blindfolds, and have everyone gather. Ask:

● **When you have good news to tell others, what do you usually do?** (Call them on the phone; write a letter; shout the news throughout my house.)

● **What kind of good news do you share?** (Losing a tooth; getting a good grade; making a sports team; being invited to a party.)

● **Do you usually wait for others to bump into you before you tell them your good news? Why or why not?** (No, I like to share good news right away; yes, I don't want to sound as if I'm bragging.)

Say: **The news that Jesus has risen from the dead is the best news ever because it means Jesus is more powerful than death!** ✪ **The Bible shows us the way to Jesus.** (Eureka!) **The Bible tells us that if we believe that Jesus rose from the dead, we can go to heaven someday! That's great news we can share with others.**

Before kids leave, distribute any **TREASURE CHEST QUEST** Clues you've been given. When you hear your Treasure Hunt Director's signal, dismiss kids to their next Discovery Site.

As a variation of this game, you can have children remove their blindfolds as they join the linking line saying "He has risen indeed!" Later you can make the point that when we believe that Jesus has risen from the dead, we are no longer in darkness, but in the light of Jesus.

✪ **BIBLE POINT**

TREASURE CHEST QUEST

BIBLE POINT
✺ The Bible shows us the way to live.

BIBLE BASIS
Acts 27:1-44. Paul stands firm in his faith, even in a shipwreck.

After Paul came to believe in Jesus, he fervently shared the news of Jesus everywhere he went. In Jerusalem, Paul encountered a group of men who opposed his teachings. These men incited a riot, accusing Paul of teaching false doctrine and of defiling the Temple. In the confusion of the angry mob, Paul was arrested and thrown in prison. The following years included trials, death threats, confused centurions, secret transfers to other prisons, and finally a trip to Rome where Paul could plead his case before Caesar. As if Paul hadn't encountered enough trouble, his ship ran into a violent storm and was eventually shipwrecked! Throughout the ordeal, Paul's faith remained strong. He prayed with other prisoners, encouraged his captors to be courageous, and shared his faith in God with everyone on board. Even in the worst circumstances, Paul's life reflected the power of Christ's love.

Most of the children in your VBS won't encounter the kind of persecution that Paul faced. But they'll face tough decisions, peer pressure, false religions, and secular advice that will challenge their faith. That's why it's important for kids to use God's Word as their map for life, a tool to guide them through the storms and "shipwrecks" along the way. Use today's activities to show children the power in the Bible and to help them discover its usefulness in successfully navigating life's everyday trials.

Day 5

Jungle Gym Games Supplies

- ○ empty plastic bowls (1 for each Clue Crew)
- ○ Ping-Pong balls (1 for each Clue Crew)
- ○ water
- ○ drinking straws (1 for each child)
- ○ plastic tubing or an old garden hose
- ○ heavy tape (such as duct tape)
- ○ beach balls (1 for each Clue Crew)
- ○ empty plastic milk jugs (1 for each child)
- ○ 2 laundry baskets
- ○ 20 tennis balls of 2 different colors (10 tennis balls of each color)
- ○ scissors
- ○ 1 watch with a second hand

The Discovery Site

Today's games focus on the story of Paul's shipwreck. While the games are fun, they also remind children of God's care when life is difficult or scary.

As kids arrive, say: **This is the last day of Treasure Hunt Bible Adventure.** Ask:

● **What's been the best part of Treasure Hunt Bible Adventure?** Answers will vary.

● **What's the best lesson you've learned at Treasure Hunt Bible Adventure?** (That the Bible is real; that the Bible is like a treasure map; that Jesus is a great treasure.)

Say: **We'll wrap up our week at Treasure Hunt Bible Adventure with some wild games that remind us that ✸ the Bible shows us the way to live.** (Eureka!)

✸ **BIBLE POINT**

Day 5

JUNGLE GYM GAMES

Man-Overboard Tag

(Energy level: High)

Supplies
none

Setup
none

The Game

1. Choose one child to be the "Man Overboard" (or "It"), and have the rest of the children form pairs and link elbows with their partners. Explain that these pairs are Ships sailing for Rome.

🌀 **BIBLE POINT**

2. Say: **Today we're learning that 🌀 the Bible shows us the way to live.** (Eureka!) **There's a Bible story that gives a good example of the way God wants us to live. As a man named Paul was sailing to Rome, there was a huge storm. The men sailing the ship threw a lot of cargo overboard to try to save themselves and their ship. Some of them even tried to jump overboard onto smaller lifeboats so they could get away. In our game we're going to pretend that a man keeps falling off the Ships.**

If the Man Overboard tags your Ship, he or she will link arms with one end of the Ship; it doesn't matter which end. Then the other end of the Ship must "fall off the ship" or unlink arms, becoming the new Man Overboard who chases down another ship to link up with.

If you like, have the person linking up to a Ship call out, "Man Overboard!" as the other person breaks away. This will signal others that a new person is now "It." You can also add a bit more excitement to the game by having two or three children be a Man Overboard at one time. This works best in large groups.

🌀 **BIBLE POINT**

3. Play for a few minutes; then gather children and say: **Paul's life was a lot like this game—full of excitement and change. But 🌀 the Bible shows us the way to live** (Eureka!), **and Paul was faithful to God through all the twists and turns. We can live faithfully too.**

Day 5

Out to Sea
(Energy level: Low)

Supplies
- empty plastic bowls such as Cool Whip containers or large margarine tubs (1 for each Clue Crew)
- water
- Ping-Pong balls (1 for each crew)
- drinking straws

This game is best played outdoors.

Setup
- Pour water into each plastic bowl, stopping about two inches from the rim of the bowl. Float a Ping-Pong ball in each bowl. You'll need one bowl for each crew.

The Game
1. Have each crew sit in a circle around a plastic bowl.

Say: **When Paul was in the boat sailing for Rome, there was a huge storm. In this game, you're going to pretend your Ping-Pong ball is a ship and the bowl is the sea. You'll blow through straws to make a huge, bubbly storm. Let's see which crew can blow its ship out of the sea first.**

2. Give each person a drinking straw, and have kids prepare to blow into the water. Give the signal to begin, and let them start blowing.

3. When a crew blows its ship out of the sea, congratulate the crew. Then have crew leaders help you refill the water in the bowls, and play again. Try using less and less water in the bowls to see how quickly crews can get the ships out of the water with this added challenge.

4. When you're finished playing, collect the playing items and ask:
- **What do you think it was like for Paul and the others on that ship?** (Scary; wild; terrifying.)
- **Have you ever been in a situation in which you felt that way?** Allow several children to share their experiences.

Say: **I'm glad ✲ the Bible shows us the way to live.** (Eureka!) **Like Paul, we can know that no matter how frightening things are, God is in control and is watching over us.**

Field Test Findings
Kids wanted to play this game again and again to see how quickly they could blow the boat from the water. This game really encourages cooperation, so let them try often!

 **BIBLE POINT**

Snake Swap
(Energy level: Medium)

Supplies
- plastic tubing (such as surgical tubing or even garden hose)
- heavy tape (such as duct tape)
- scissors

53

Day 5

Setup

● Cut tubing into three-foot lengths. Use heavy tape to fasten the ends of each length together, forming a circle. These represent snakes. If you like, use a permanent marker to draw the head and eyes of the snake as if it is biting down on its own tail. You'll need one "snake" for every crew.

The Game

1. Say: **After the storm, Paul was shipwrecked on the island of Malta. He was gathering wood for a fire there when a snake clamped onto his hand! Paul shook the snake off into the fire, and he wasn't hurt.**

   We would surely find snakes in the jungle, so we're going to play a game called Snake Swap.

2. Have crew members form circles and hold hands. Show children the rubber snakes and say: **Let's pretend these are snakes, biting down on their own tails to make circles. I'm going to put one around the neck of one person in each crew. When I say "go," you must pass the snake from neck to neck without using any hands. You'll have to figure out how to get a second person's head into the circle, get the first person's head out, then pass it on to the next person. When the snake has made its way back to the neck of the person it started with, everyone will shout out, "The Bible shows us the way to live!" and sit down.**

3. Put a snake on the neck of one person in each crew. Make sure all crews are still holding hands; then give the signal to go. Cheer on the crews, encouraging them to get that snake off their necks! Initiate a big round of applause when all crews have accomplished their task, and play again if time allows.

4. Gather the snakes and say: **Even when Paul was in scary situations such as storms, having snakes bite him, or being held captive, he knew that God loved him and would do what was best for him. When we get into scary situations, we can remember that** ✪ **the Bible shows us the way to live** (Eureka!) **and we can trust God to watch over us.**

A CLUE FOR YOU!

You may need to encourage kids to kneel or even lie down as they move the snake from one person to another. This is a super game for getting kids to solve problems creatively!

✪ BIBLE POINT

Field Test Findings

Our Jungle Gym Games Leader was in a hurry to test this game, so he didn't take the time to set up a course; he used one that was already there! A line of trees outside made an ideal (and easy) course for kids to "sail" through!

Crash Course

(Energy level: High)

Supplies

● beach balls (1 for each Clue Crew)
● various obstacles to place in your playing area
● 1 watch with a second hand

Setup

● Create several identical obstacle courses in your playing area. The courses might require going under a chair, around a pylon, over a large brick, and so on. Ideally, you should have one course for each crew.

Day 5

The Game

1. Say: **When Paul was sailing to Rome, he encountered a terrible storm. The ship had to go around islands and other dangerous obstacles. In this game we're going to pretend these beach balls are Paul's ship. Your crew must guide Paul's ship through all the obstacles it faced during the storm.**

2. Demonstrate how each child must roll the ball along the ground to guide it through the course. Show kids the order of the obstacles and what must be done at each stop along the way. Say: **After getting your ship through the obstacles, push it back to the starting line and pass it on to the next person in your Clue Crew.**

3. Have crews line up at the starting point. Give the first person in each line a beach ball. Begin the race. If you have more crews than obstacle courses, time crews as they go through the course. When the first round of crews has finished, encourage them to cheer for the second round of crews. Compare times at the end, and congratulate members of the crew with the fastest time for being such great sailors!

4. Collect the balls and ask:

● **What hard things—or obstacles—do you face in life?** (Tests; when my friends move; telling people about Jesus.)

● **How does the Bible guide you through those times?** (It gives me advice; it tells me what people in the Bible did when things were hard for them; it reminds me that God loves me no matter what.)

Say: **The Bible shows us the way to live** (Eureka!) **It's sort of like a treasure map for our lives. When life seems stormy or we have to do hard things, we can look to God's Word for help.**

Cargo Toss

(Energy level: High)

Supplies
● empty plastic milk jugs
● 2 laundry baskets
● 20 tennis balls of 2 different colors (10 tennis balls of each color)

Setup
● Cut each milk jug around the middle about two inches below the handle. Discard the bottom half. The remaining half forms a plastic scoop in which children can catch balls. You'll need one scoop for each child.
● Place one laundry basket at each end of the playing area.

The Game
1. Form two teams, and have all kids stand in the center of the playing area.

Field Test Findings

We were originally going to have kids push the balls with brooms. But when we were short on brooms, our Jungle Gym Games Leader improvised and found that hands work just as well (plus, they're easier to find!).

✹ BIBLE POINT

A CLUE FOR YOU!

If tennis balls are not available in two colors, place a strip of brightly colored tape around half of the balls to differentiate them from the others.

Day 5

Say: **When Paul was on the ship, there was a terrible storm. One thing the soldiers and sailors did to try to save themselves was toss cargo overboard. In this game, we're going to pretend we're throwing cargo overboard and trying to land it in our lifeboats.**

2. Give each child a plastic scoop. Determine which team will be using which color of tennis balls. Say: **The goal is to get all of your cargo (tennis balls) into your team's lifeboat (laundry basket). You may pick up or catch cargo only with your scoop; you may not touch the balls with your hands or other body parts. And remember, a storm is raging the whole time, so you'll have trouble walking. This means you can take only five steps before you have to toss the cargo. You'll be trying to catch your team's cargo and pass it along to other crew members to your lifeboat. You'll also be trying to catch the cargo of the other team and toss it away from its lifeboat.**

3. Toss all the balls high into the air so kids can start catching them. Make sure that kids take only five steps before passing the balls on to their teammates. When one team has gotten all its cargo into its lifeboat, stop the game, gather all the balls, and play again!

4. When the game is over, collect the balls and plastic scoops. Gather the children and say: **The men on the ship must have been terrified during that storm. But Paul trusted God to take care of them. He tried to encourage others on the ship not to be afraid and to trust in God.** ✹ **The Bible shows us the way to live** (Eureka!) **through the example of Paul and others.**

Before kids leave, distribute any **TREASURE CHEST QUEST** Clues you've been given. When you hear your Treasure Hunt Director's signal, dismiss kids to their next Discovery Site.

A CLUE FOR YOU!

If playing this game outdoors, crews may be tempted to toss the tennis balls of other crews very far away. If this becomes a problem, specify that if the balls are tossed outside a specific boundary (such as past the trees or beyond the swing sets), players on that team may take only three steps before tossing a ball. This will encourage players to toss the balls within the boundaries of the playing area.

✹ **BIBLE POINT**

TREASURE CHEST QUEST